SKIN

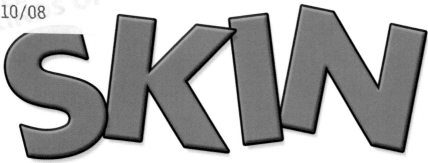

Sara Swan Miller

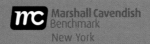
Marshall Cavendish
Benchmark
New York

Marshall Cavendish Benchmark
99 White Plains Road
Tarrytown, New York 10591-9001
www.marshallcavendish.us

All Web sites were available and accurate when this book was sent to press.

Editor: Doug Sanders
Publisher: Michelle Bisson
Art Director: Anahid Hamparian
Series Designer: Alex Ferrari

Library of Congress Cataloging-in-Publication Data

Miller, Sara Swan.
  Skin / Sara Swan Miller.
      p. cm. — (All kinds of...)
  Summary: "An exploration of the skin and various outer coverings found in
the animal world"—Provided by publisher.
  Includes bibliographical references and index.
  ISBN-13: 978-0-7614-2713-1
  1. Skin—Juvenile literature. I. Title. II. Series.

  QL941.M57 2007
  573.5—dc22

                              2006030721

Photo research by Candlepants Incorporated

Cover photo: Chris Windsor / Getty Images

The photographs in this book are used by permission and through the courtesy of:
Peter Arnold Inc.: BIOS Denis-Huot M. & C., 1; Michael Fairchild, 34; BIOS Klien & Hubert, 22. *Corbis:* Jens Nieth/zefa, 4; Michael & Patricia Fogden, 10; Volkmar Brockhaus/zefa, 14; Charles Krebs, 43. *Getty Images:* Wolf Fahrenbach, 7; Tom Morrison, 8. *Photo Researchers Inc.:* Anatomical Travelogue, 9; Eye of Science, 16. *Minden Pictures:* Piotr Naskrecki, 12; Norbert Wu, 15; Mark Spencer/Auscape, 18; Chris Newbert, 20, 21; Pete Oxford, 25, 29; Christian Ziegler, 26; Ingo Arndt/Foto Natura, 27 (inset); Thomas Mangelsen, 27; Richard Du Toit, 31; Frans Lanting, 32; Tim Fitzharris, 36; Jan Vermeer/Foto Natura, 37; Michael Quinton, 38; SA Team/Foto Natura, 41; Gerry Ellis, 42; Heidi & Hans Jurgen Koch, 44.

Printed in Malaysia
1 3 5 6 4 2

CONTENTS

*Our skin helps protect us
and keep our insides in.*

SKIN DEEP

Did you know that your skin is an organ? It is actually your largest organ. It covers your whole body, like a soft thin suit of armor. Skin does many important things for us. First of all, it helps hold everything together and, along with layers of muscle, it keeps our insides inside. It is our first defense against germs. Without the tough shield of our skin, bacteria would easily get in and attack the rest of our bodies. Skin protects us from too much cold or heat, keeps us from drying out, and is home to our sense of touch. Skin also resists water and

WHAT'S THAT SMELL?

You may have noticed that if you do not wash often, you can start to smell bad. It is not actually the dirt on your skin that makes you smell. The odor is caused by tiny microbes that live on the surface of the skin. They eat all kinds of tinier things, including other microbes. They are constantly leaving their waste matter on the skin. After several days, the wastes build up and give off a nasty smell. That is one reason why it is important to wash. Too much washing, however, can remove the oils from the skin and make it too dry.

protects us from getting soggy inside when we take a bath.

Skin is made up of three layers. The outer layer, the one you can see, is the *epidermis*. At the bottom of the epidermis new skin cells are constantly forming. As they grow, they move toward the top of the epidermis. This takes two to three weeks. The new cells push the older cells to the surface, where they die. The skin you see on your body is really made up of dead cells.

The dead cells are filled with *keratin*, a tough protein. It is the same material that fingernails are made of. The dead cells are like a coat, protecting the ones below from damage. Dead cells flake off constantly and are replaced by new ones. Every minute we lose about 30,000 to 40,000. Most of the cells in the epidermis are busy making new skin cells. Other cells found there make a substance called *melanin*. Melanin gives your skin its color. The more melanin you have, the darker your skin is. In bright sunlight, these cells make more melanin to help keep your skin from burning. That is why, if you spend a lot of time in the sun, your skin tans or changes color.

The next layer under the epidermis is the *dermis*. Oil glands, sweat glands, blood vessels, and nerve endings are all found there. The dermis also contains a lot of *collagen* and *elastin,* proteins that make your skin both firm and stretchy.

The oil glands, which are also called *sebaceous glands,* produce an oil called *sebum*. It rises to the sur-

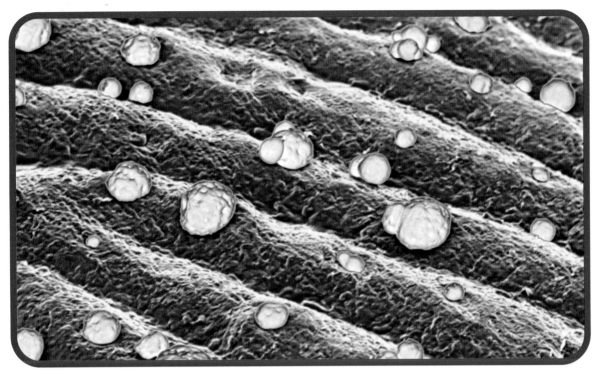

A close-up look at a fingertip, showing ridges and drops of sweat.

face of the epidermis and keeps the skin moist and protected from bacteria. It is also the substance that makes your skin water resistant.

The dermis also produces sweat. It comes up through little pores, or openings, in the top of the skin. When the sweat joins with the sebum, it makes a protective, sticky film. Sweat also helps us stay cool. When it is very hot, the sweat glands in the dermis produce extra sweat. As it evaporates, or turns from liquid to gas form, it helps us cool down.

Blood vessels in the dermis bring oxygen and nutrients to the skin cells and help keep them healthy. The blood vessels also carry away the waste products the cells create. The blood vessels in the skin help us stay at just the right temperature. When you start to get too hot, the blood vessels bring warm blood closer to the surface to cool the area. When it is very cold outside, the blood vessels get smaller and narrower and keep the warm blood away from the surface of the skin.

The dermis is full of nerve endings that give you your sense of touch. They also protect you from getting hurt. For instance, if you touch something very hot, the nerve endings send a message to the brain. In a flash, the brain then sends a message to the muscles to snatch your hand away.

The third layer of skin is called the *subcutaneous layer.* It is made mostly of fat and helps keep your body

Nerve endings under the skin give us our sense of touch.

warm. It is also the layer where the roots of your hair are found. The hairs grow out of little tubes in the skin called *follicles* and up through the dermis. You may not think of yourself as particularly hairy, but you have hair follicles all over your body. The only places where you have none are your palms, the soles of your feet, and your lips. Some places on your body have more follicles than others. On your head, for example, you have about 100,000 follicles.

A close-up look at a hair growing out of a follicle.

Skin is a remarkable thing. It helps protect not only people, but other animals too. Many mammals have outer coverings similar to our own. Other animals have different kinds of outsides. Let's find out more about the various kinds of skin, scales, feathers, and fur found in the natural world.

This adult cicada is molting, breaking out of its old exoskeleton.

INSECT ARMOR

An insect's outer body is very different from ours. Instead of soft skin, it has a hard shell called an *exoskeleton,* meaning "outer skeleton." An insect's muscles are attached to this strong exoskeleton in place of the bones that would otherwise be found inside an animal's body. The exoskeleton protects an insect from predators and acts as a waterproof shield that keeps it from drying out.

With a hard shell on the outside, how does an insect grow? Some insects go through incomplete metamorphosis. They hatch from the egg looking very much like a small adult, but without wings. As one of these insects grows in stages from larva to adult, the exoskeleton splits open and a larger version of the same insect emerges. It leaves its old exoskeleton behind. This is called *molting.* The problem for the insect, however, is that it takes time for the new exoskeleton to harden. While it is still soft, the insect is not well

MANY MOLTS
Most insects that undergo incomplete metamorphosis molt four to eight times. But some insects may molt twenty times before they become adults.

OTHER ARTHROPODS

Insects are *arthropods,* which means "jointed feet." All arthropods have exoskeletons. There are many different kinds of arthropods. Spiders, mites, scorpions, and other arachnids are all arthropods. So are millipedes and centipedes. Still others include crabs, lobsters, and barnacles. Most of them breathe through openings in their exoskeletons, although some, such as lobsters, breathe with gills. Others, such as some spiders, have a simple form of lungs.

As arthropods grow, they have to molt several times. Lobsters, for instance, may molt up to twenty-five times in the seven years it takes them to grow to full size. A hermit crab may molt as many as six times a year when it is young. When it gets to a certain size, though, it does not molt as often.

The spines on a spiny spider's exoskeleton help protect it from hungry birds and lizards.

protected from predators. It is a brief and dangerous time before the insect has its tough armor once again. When an insect becomes an adult, though, it stops molting.

Most insects, such as butterflies, go through complete metamorphosis. When a butterfly egg hatches, a caterpillar comes out. It looks very different from an adult butterfly. As it grows, it molts several times. Then it forms a chrysalis around itself and goes through a complete change before becoming an adult butterfly. After that, the butterfly does not molt again.

An insect's exoskeleton is good for more than just protecting it from predators and the weather. This outer covering lets the insect breathe. The outside of an insect's body is lined with small openings called *spiracles*. Air enters through the spiracles and travels through breathing tubes that go all through its body.

An insect's exoskeleton helps it in other ways. The exoskeleton has a variety of sense organs that detect light, sound, pressure, temperature, and wind.

Insect exoskeletons come in all different colors and patterns. Often these colors and patterns match the surroundings the insects live in, so they are well camouflaged. They blend in and are not easily seen. Katydids are some of the best camouflaged insects. They spend their lives in the trees, and their green, curved bodies make them look just like leaves. Many moths are also well camouflaged. During the day, most rest on tree trunks. The pattern on their wings blends perfectly with the bark.

Some camouflaged moths have other tricks they use to blend in and stay safe. The ones known as underwings have brightly colored back wings. When the moths are resting, their underwings are hidden beneath their dull-colored outer wings. Blocking or covering their brighter colors keeps them safe. But if a hungry bird approaches,

This moth uses camouflage to try and blend in and to protect itself.

the moth suddenly spreads its wings and takes flight. The flash of its underwings startles the bird, and the moth flies away to safety.

Insects that are eaten by other creatures are not the only ones that use camouflage. Many predator insects do too. A praying mantis, for example, is a master of disguise. An American praying mantis is green and brown, matching the color of the grasses it waits among. It sits very still. When an insect passes under its nose, the praying mantis grabs it and quickly gobbles it up.

One good way to protect yourself, if you are a harmless insect, is to be colored like a much fiercer one. For instance, several kinds of insects look like stinging bees

WAITING IN AMBUSH
Ambush bugs are camouflaged in yellow and brown, matching the goldenrod flowers they perch on, waiting for prey.

and wasps. Bee flies, hover flies, and flower flies are not able to sting but have the colors and patterns that make them look like stinging insects.

A viceroy butterfly has another way to protect itself. It looks almost identical to a monarch butterfly. As a cater-pillar, a monarch feeds on bad-tasting milkweed plants. This diet makes the caterpillars and then the adult butter-flies taste bad. Birds will try to stay away from any butterfly that looks like a monarch, so the viceroy butter-fly benefits from resembling its foul-tasting relative.

Some insects have markings that can fool their predators. An eyed elater beetle has big eyespots on its back. A predator thinks they are the eyes of a much big-ger animal and leaves the beetle alone. A polyphemus moth has somewhat similar markings. It has bright black-and-yellow eyespots on its back wings. When it is at rest, it blends in with the bark, but when it is startled, the moth flashes its scary eyespots.

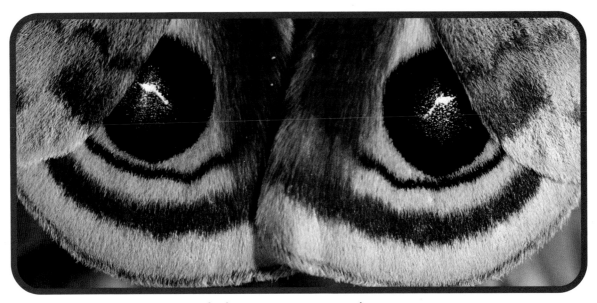

An io moth's eyespots help scare away predators.

A close-up look at a shark's scales.

3

FISHES: SCALY, SMOOTH, OR BONY

A fish's skin is well suited to life in a watery world. Most fishes are covered with thin scales. The scales grow out of the epidermis, in rows, and are made mostly of an element called calcium. In most fishes the scales overlap like the shingles on a roof. They protect the fish from injury and disease.

Sharks and rays have different kinds of scales. Their bodies are covered with jagged, tooth-like scales that make their bodies feel rough to the touch.

Other fishes, such as gars, have scales that are flat and squarish. They hardly overlap at all.

Scutes are bony plates that are shield-like versions of scales. Many sardines have a single row of scutes between the paired fins on their belly. This helps protect their undersides. The well-named pineconefish has hard, ridged scutes all over its body.

Some fishes have no scales. Most catfishes, for instance, have smooth, scaleless bodies. But some species have hard, bony plates that protect them. Other species have sharp spines in some of their fins that help ward off predators.

Sea horses have no scales either. Instead, their bodies are covered with skin stretched over the bony ridges that form rings around their bodies. Scientists identify different species of sea horses by counting the rings. Having body armor helps protect a sea horse from predators, but it means that it cannot bend its body much to help it swim. Instead, a sea horse swims upright and flutters its small fins to get around.

LEAF COVER

A leafy seadragon, a relative of the sea horses, has leafy flaps of skin that trail in the water and look like floating seaweed.

A leafy seadragon can be hard to spot among the seaweed.

Fishes' scales are just one form of protection. Their skin also creates a mucus that covers the scales. Chemicals in the mucus help kill bacteria. The covering also lets a fish swim more easily through the water and helps it slip quickly away when it is caught by a predator.

When it comes to producing mucus, a hagfish is the champion. This scaleless fish creates a huge amount of slime that turns predators away. A 31-inch-long (79-centimeter) North American hagfish can make enough slime to fill a bucket in one minute.

A fish's skin does more than just protect it. It also helps a fish taste. A fish has taste organs in the skin on its head, fins, and lips, as well as in its mouth. It can taste food in the water well before it takes it into its mouth.

A fish has other sense organs called *lateral lines* just under its skin. These are fluid-filled tubes that run over the head and along both sides of the body. Special cells inside pick up vibrations through pores in the skin. A fish uses its lateral lines to sense the direction of water currents and the presence of nearby objects, predators, or prey. Fish also need their lateral lines in order to sense sounds. Picking up vibrations, the lateral lines help a school of fish stay together. These special sense organs also help a fish find its way at night or when the water is murky.

Fish come in all kinds of colors. Some are quite drab, while others are as colorful as a butterfly. Fish colors come mostly from pigments in the skin, but also from light shining off other substances in the skin.

A clownfish is safe among the stinging tentacles of a sea anemone.

Many fishes are well camouflaged. A flounder, for example, lies flat on the ocean floor, and the pattern and color of its skin help it to blend in with the pebbles and sand. A flounder can even change color to match its surroundings. Would-be predators usually pass it by.

Toadfishes are predators that use camouflage to trap their prey. A common toadfish, for example, has a sandy white body covered with brown spots. It lies perfectly still, blending in with the sea floor. When a possible meal swims close enough, the toadfish darts forward and seizes it.

A clownfish, on the other hand, is brightly colored in orange, white, and black. It does not need camouflage because it lives among the stinging tentacles, or arms, of a sea anemone. Other fishes do not dare to come near an anemone, but the clownfish is able to swim among the tentacles without triggering the anemone's stinging cells.

Some fishes mimic others with their colors and patterns. The mimic blenny looks almost identical to another fish called the cleaner wrasse. The cleaner wrasse makes a living by cleaning parasites off the bodies of other fishes, which do not mind having such a helper around. The blenny, however, is a fierce predator. Looking like the cleaner wrasse, the blenny can swim right up to another fish and easily nip off bits of its prey.

A cleaner wrasse goes to work on the gills of a much larger fish.

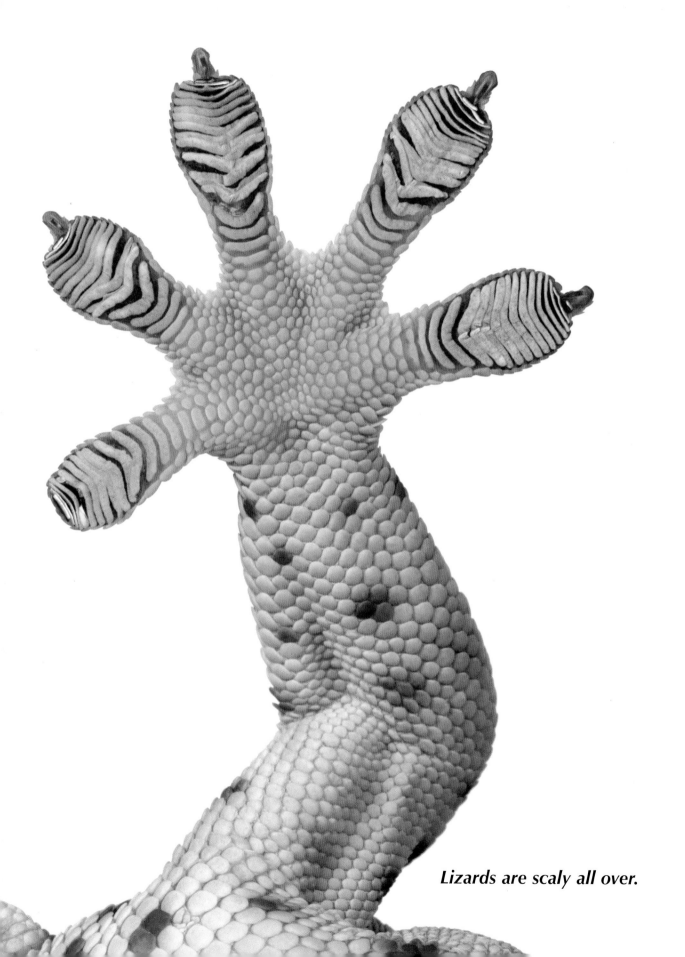

Lizards are scaly all over.

AMPHIBIAN AND REPTILE SKINS

Amphibians and reptiles have many things in common, but their skins are quite different. Amphibians have thin, moist skin and no scales. Reptiles have thick skin covered with scales.

A salamander's moist skin has two layers. The outer layer, or epidermis, protects the tissues underneath. Beneath this layer is the dermis, which has many blood vessels, nerves, and glands. Some of the glands make mucus, which covers the entire salamander and keeps it moist. Salamanders breathe largely through their skin, so if the skin dries out, they will die. Some kinds, the lungless salamanders, breathe entirely through their skin.

Salamanders do not drink with their mouths, but through their skin. They sit in a puddle or in wet sand or mud and absorb, or draw in, the water.

The dermis in some salamanders has glands that make poison. Poisonous salamanders are usually brightly colored.

HANDLE WITH CARE!

Salamander skin is very sensitive. If you want to pick up a salamander, wash your hands first and make sure they are wet.

Their bright colors send a warning to predators: Don't eat me! A red eft, the young version of the kind of salamander called a newt, is bright orange with black dots. It spends about three years on land, well protected from predators. But when it becomes an adult, it returns to a pond. There its skin turns a drab olive green.

The Californian newt is another poisonous salamander. Its back is a drab brown, but its belly is a bright yellow-orange. When a predator comes near, the newt raises its tail and head and flashes its bright underside. The predator better not try to eat this salamander. Its poison is so strong that it could kill a fox.

Most salamanders are dark and well camouflaged with their various spots or stripes. They hide among the moist, dead leaves on the forest floor.

As they grow, salamanders shed their skin. Some shed as often as once a week. When they are done, they eat the dead skin.

Like a salamander, a frog is covered with thin, moist skin made up of two layers—the epidermis and

MISTER WRINKLES

Someone once said that a hellbender looks more like a bad dream than like a living creature. This large salamander has deeply wrinkled, slimy skin that looks as if it is several sizes too large. A hellbender spends most of its time in fast-moving streams where there is plenty of oxygen. The hellbender has no lungs, so it breathes entirely through its skin. The wrinkles help absorb oxygen because they provide more surface area.

the dermis. The dermis is full of blood vessels, which can absorb or take in oxygen from the skin. Underwater, frogs breathe entirely through their skin. On land, they also breathe with their simple, sac-like lungs.

A frog can breathe through its thin mucus-covered skin.

Most frogs are camouflaged by their brown or green skins. Pickerel frogs, wood frogs, and green frogs, for instance, blend into the background of grass and mud.

There are also several frogs whose bright colors warn predators that they are highly poisonous. They may be red, bright blue, or bright yellow and black. The golden poison frog of South America has enough poison in its skin to kill one hundred people! Native peoples discovered how poisonous this frog's skin really is. They heat the tips of their blowgun darts, then wipe them on a frog's back. That gives the hunters a deadly weapon for striking down small prey.

A toad's skin is usually drier than the moist skin of a frog. The toad's outer covering is not smooth like a frog's, but covered with warts. People used to think that they could get warts from holding a toad, but that is a myth.

Toads do have poison glands, called *parotoid glands,* behind their eyes. Some toads release poison through glands on their backs that might cause a rash. Others, including the American toad, can actually squirt the poison out of their parotoid glands.

Most toads are camouflaged in brownish olive with some darker spots here and there. When they sit still, most predators will not notice them.

Unlike amphibians such as salamanders, frogs, and toads, lizards are reptiles and covered with scales. Their scales come in different types. Some lizards, such as collared lizards, have small scales like little grains. Other lizards, such as gila monsters, have bead-shaped scales. Most lizards have scales that are large and plate-like. Some scales are smooth, while others have ridges called

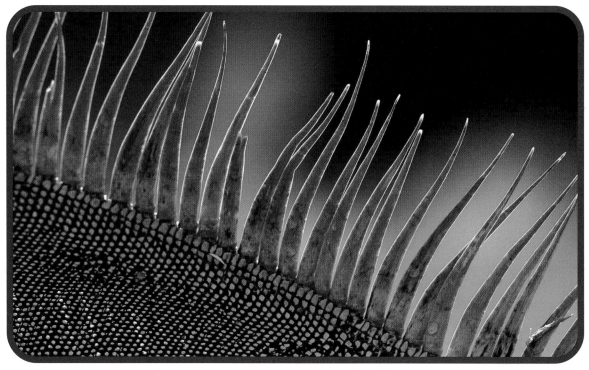

A green iguana has protective spines on its back.

keels. The Texas horned lizards have scales that have developed into spines. Scales are perfect protection for animals that live in dry, hot places. The scales shield the skin from the sun and keep the body from drying out.

Many lizards use camouflage. Basilisks and flying lizards live in the trees and are leaf green. Both thorny devils and knob-tailed geckos live in the desert, and their skin is a spotted brown. Other lizards are more brightly colored, including the poisonous gila monster, which has bold patterns. Many lizards turn bright colors at mating time. The male marine iguana, for instance, which is usually black, changes to bright red, black, and blue.

Chameleons are lizards that are known for changing colors to match their background. It turns out that camouflage is not the reason for their color changes. The color

A close-up view of a panther chameleon's scales.

shifts have more to do with light, temperature, and mood. When it is cold, a chameleon will turn darker, absorbing or drawing in more heat. When it is warm, the chameleon is a lighter hue. Fear will also make a chameleon change color, usually to black. Chameleons communicate with one another using color, especially at mating time. Both male and female panther chameleons put on bold displays of yellow, red, green, orange, and blue.

Like lizards, snakes are covered with scales. The scales on their back are rather small, but the ones on their belly are large. Snakes use these belly scales to pull themselves along by catching and holding on to rough surfaces. The scales on the back usually have a smooth, shiny look, but sometimes they are dull and rough. Water snakes have scales with ridges, or keels, that help them swim. Snakes that live or hunt in underground burrows, however, have smooth scales that help them move easily through the soil.

Many snakes use camouflage. The stripes on a garter snake's body help it blend in with the sticks and grass it lives among. Boa constrictors are marked with patches of brown, tan, gray, or green. They lie in trees among leaves and branches, waiting for their prey to come close enough to grab.

Some poisonous snakes, however, are brightly colored. The highly poisonous coral snakes have bright red, yellow, and black stripes. Several other non-venomous snakes mimic, or copy, this pattern. The New Mexico milk snake, the organpipe shovelnosed snake, the scarlet king snake, the scarlet snake, and the central plains milk

This emerald tree boa stays very still, coiled on a branch.

snake all have similar bright stripes. Would-be predators of these copycat snakes are fooled, but many people have learned to tell the difference. The coral snake has a black snout, not a red or yellow one like most of its mimics, and each of its red bands is bordered by two yellow bands. To remember that, people often use this rhyme: "Red touch yellow, kill a fellow; red touch black, friend of Jack."

When it comes to turtles, the most obvious thing about their outsides is the shell. The top shell is called a *carapace*, and the bottom one is called a *plastron*. Both halves are part of the bony skeleton. The outer surface of the shell is covered by the epidermis, a thin layer of skin containing blood vessels and nerves. Over the skin are horny scales, called scutes, made of keratin. They protect the soft epidermis. Turtles shed their scutes from time to time, and new ones grow in.

A few species of turtles do not have horny plates on their shells. Softshell turtles have thin shells covered by a thick, leathery skin. Leatherback turtles have a thick leathery covering too.

By and large, turtles make use of camouflage. Many have patterns that blend in with their surroundings. Others have solid colors that match the background tones of the places where they live.

Alligators and crocodiles are also covered with scutes. They are much harder and thicker than other reptiles'. The scutes on an alligator's back are incredibly tough. They are almost like armor, and it is nearly impossible for a predator to bite through them. They include grains of bone called *osteoderms*. The scutes on the

A Nile crocodile is known for its tough scales.

belly have fewer osteoderms and thus are much softer.

The leathery skins of alligators and crocodiles have caused them a lot of trouble in the past. People sought them for making shoe and belt leather. There was so much demand that many species were on the verge of extinction, never to be seen on earth again. Now laws protect alligators and crocodiles, and they are growing in number.

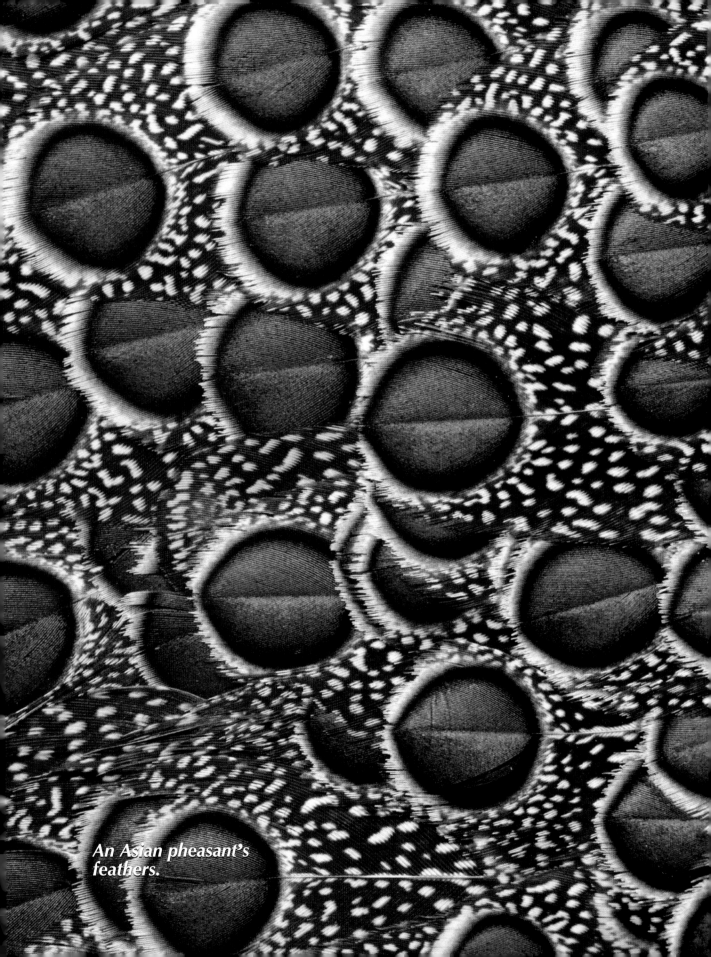
An Asian pheasant's feathers.

5

BIRD FEATHERS

All birds have feathers. Birds are almost completely covered with them, although most birds do not have feathers on their legs and feet. Even birds that cannot fly have feathers. There are six different kinds of feathers: contour feathers, flight feathers, down feathers, filoplumes, semiplumes, and bristles.

Contour feathers cover most of a bird's body. They protect a bird from rain, wind, sun, and some types of injury. The flight feathers are the large ones on the wings and tail. Those on the wings provide power and lift when a bird flies. The tail feathers act as brakes and help the bird steer.

Under the contour feathers are down feathers. They are soft and fluffy and trap air next to the skin. They keep a bird warm and protect it from heat and cold. Some down feathers are called powder down feathers.

NICE AND WARM
Birds that stay in chilly northern regions in the winter do not get cold partly because they are wearing little "down jackets."

When they wear out, they form a fine powder. A bird can spread this powder over its feathers to waterproof them. The powder also helps a bird clean its feathers.

Filoplumes are fine hair-like feathers. Scientists think they may help a bird sense air pressure and then adjust its flight feathers in response.

Semiplumes are longer than down feathers and almost as fluffy. They help provide shape and warmth under the contour feathers.

Bristle feathers look like the bristles on a brush. These small feathers are usually found around a bird's eyelids, nostrils, and bill. They are sensitive to touch.

Feathers are made of keratin. The base of a feather

Crested cranes have a crown of bristles on the top of their heads.

grows out of a follicle in the skin. Each contour feather and flight feather has a lot of hair-like *barbs* that are joined together with little hooks. They act like a zipper, giving the feather a smooth surface and making it strong enough to face heavy winds. Sometimes the hooks may come apart. Then a bird will preen its feathers by running them through its bill to reattach the hooks.

LITTLE DINOSAURS

Scientists believe that birds descended from a kind of dinosaur. Unlike other reptiles, dinosaurs' legs were right under their bodies, not splayed out to the side. For this reason, dinosaurs are called "bird hipped." As for bird feathers, they evolved from dinosaur scales. Most birds still have scales on their legs. Only owls' legs are covered with soft feathers.

Birds lose their feathers from time to time and grow new ones. This is called molting. Most birds molt a little at a time, often over several months, so they will have enough feathers to provide warmth and allow them to fly. A few species, though, lose many of their feathers at once, and so cannot fly for a short time during molting. Most birds molt once a year, usually when the seasons change. North American songbirds molt when the days get shorter in the early fall. Some songbirds molt twice a year, in the fall and right after breeding. The males lose their bright colors, which helps them blend in better and stay safer from predators.

After breeding, before a bird begins to sit on its eggs, patches of feathers on the stomach fall out. The bare spots are called *brood patches*. They are full of blood vessels, which warm the eggs while they develop. Without brood patches, heat from the parent's body could not reach the eggs, because the feathers would get in the way.

Bird feathers come in all different colors. Some birds have really bright plumage. Think of the brilliant colors of parrots or toucans. Other birds are camouflaged in colors and patterns that match the place where they live and help protect them from predators. The color in the feathers comes mostly from pigments. Birds can make most of these pigments, but not all. Certain pigments, called *carotenoids*, create red, orange, and yellow and can only come through a bird's food. If a flamingo, for instance, doesn't get to eat certain shrimp and other crustaceans, it will lose its pink or orange color. Some colors in birds also come from light bouncing off special structures in the feathers.

Flamingoes get their pink color from the foods they eat.

An eagle owl's feathers keep it warm in the snow.

Among songbirds, the males are usually more brightly colored than the females. A male scarlet tanager, for example, is bright orange-red with black wings. The female is a drab yellow-green with dusky wings. A male American goldfinch is bright yellow with black wings. The female is olive colored.

It makes sense for the males to be more colorful than the females. It is a male's job to court the female and to drive away other males. His bright colors help in this goal. It is usually the female's job to sit on the eggs and protect them and keep them warm. Her drab colors help camouflage her while she sits on the nest.

Feathers help a bird fly and stay warm. They protect it from the rain, snow, sun, and wind. They also help a male attract a female at courtship time. Feathers have many important jobs.

Some of a porcupine's hairs are sharp quills.

6

MAMMAL FUR AND MORE

When you think of a mammal, you probably picture an animal covered with hair. Not every mammal is hairy, but they all have at least some hair at some time in their lives.

The glands that give off the oil that coats a mammal's hair are found near the follicles. A special small muscle may be next to the follicle as well. When it tightens, the hair stands up straight. You may have noticed that when a dog is angry, the hairs on its back stand up. This is a signal to other creatures to "Stay away!"

The fur coat of most mammals is made up of different kinds of hair. On the outside are the *guard hairs*, which protect the fur underneath. In some mammals, including porcupines and hedgehogs, some guard hairs have turned into hard spines. Others have formed bristles,

YOU CAN'T RUB A MOLE THE WRONG WAY

Whether a mole is going forward or backward in its tunnel, its thick, flexible fur will be pushed flat.

which are long firm hairs that grow constantly, such as those in a lion's mane or a horse's tail. Others are called *awns*. They do not keep growing and have a wider tip. They are shorter than guard hairs. Under the guard hairs and awn hairs is a fine, soft layer of hair called the *undercoat*. The undercoat helps keep a mammal warm.

Most mammals also have special hairs called whiskers. They grow mostly around the nostrils or other areas of the face. They are found on other parts of some animals as well. Cats and squirrels, for example, have whiskers on their ankles. Manatees have them all over their bodies.

The whiskers help a mammal feel and sense the world around it. Each whisker grows out of a special follicle that is sealed by a capsule of blood. This is called a *blood sinus*. When a whisker touches something, it bends and pushes the blood to one side or the other. This allows the nerve cells to sense when the whiskers touch something. They especially help a mammal feel its way in the dark.

Mammals, like birds, molt from time to time. Some mammals, including humans and some breeds of dogs, molt all the time. Hairs are constantly being replaced a few at a time. Other mammals molt at certain seasons, with all the hair being replaced more or less at once. Weasels and many other arctic mammals replace their brown summer fur with white fur, which helps them stay camouflaged in the snow.

A mammal's hair color is due to proteins called

An ocelot's long whiskers help it find its way through tight spots.

melanins. Some hairs are dark, and some are pale. Most mammals' fur is brown, black, or white. No mammals have fur as brightly colored as the feathers of most birds. Perhaps the most colorful mammal is the golden lion tamarin. Its fur is a bright yellow color.

Most mammals use camouflage. A giraffe's splotchy fur helps it blend in with the leaves. A cheetah's spotted

A cheetah's coat helps it blend in with the African plains.

fur helps it blend in with the leaves. A cheetah's spotted coat camouflages it in the tall, dry grass. Although it may not seem so at first, a zebra's black and white stripes also work as camouflage. A lion, its main predator, must focus on a single animal in a herd in order to catch it. A herd of striped zebras running at the same time confuses lions and other predators, making it hard to pick out a single zebra.

Some mammals have hardly any hair. They depend on their skin for protection. Manatees, walruses, whales, elephants, naked mole rats, and rhinos are nearly hairless. Aardvarks have very tough skins, but little hair.

Other mammals have different kinds of body coverings besides hair. A pangolin, for example, is covered

An elephant's skin is nearly hairless and very tough.

with tough, overlapping scales. It looks like a pinecone with legs. An armadillo is covered with plates that act like armor. A three-banded armadillo can curl itself into a ball for protection, with only its hard plates showing.

Besides hair, the other thing that is unique to mammals is that they all have *mammary glands* in their skin. All female mammals feed their young milk made by their mammary glands. Humans have just one pair of mammary glands, but some mammals have as many as eleven pairs. Mammals that give birth to larger numbers of babies at once usually have several pairs of mammary glands.

This armadillo is well armored, covered with many plates.

Mammals have other glands in their skin as well. Most mammals have sweat glands, which help cool the animal and carry away wastes. Some mammals have bodies almost entirely covered with sweat glands. Think of the way a horse sweats after it has run a race. Other mammals have sweat glands only in certain places. Some rodents and carnivores have sweat glands only in their feet. Whales and some bats have no sweat glands at all.

Some mammals also have scent glands and musk glands. The scents may be used to mark a mammal's territory or to help find a mate. Musk glands can also be used for protection, particularly by skunks. When you see a skunk stomping its front legs and waving its tail, you know it is about to spray a foul-smelling liquid at you. You also know it is time to run!

PLATYPUSES AND ECHIDNAS

Almost all mammals have nipples on their bellies or chests that give off milk from the mammary glands. The newborns grasp onto the nipples with their mouths and suck the milk. But platypuses and echidnas are different. They have no nipples at all. The milk just flows from pores on their belly. The newborns suck and lap the milk from their mother's fur.

GLOSSARY

arthropod—A type of animal, such as an insect, arachnid, or crustacean, whose name means "joint footed."

awn—A type of hair, shorter than a guard hair and longer than a down hair.

barb—A hair-like part of a feather.

blood sinus—A capsule of blood at the base of a whisker.

brood patch—A bare spot on a bird's belly that helps it keep its eggs warm.

carapace—The upper part of a turtle's shell.

carotenoid—A pigment that creates red, orange, and yellow.

collagen—A protein that makes skin firm.

dermis—The middle layer of a mammal's skin.

elastin—A protein that makes skin elastic.

epidermis—The top layer of a mammal's skin.

exoskeleton—The hard outer layer of an arthropod.

follicle—A tube-like structure in the skin from which hair grows.

guard hairs—A protective layer covering the undercoat.

keratin—A tough protein of which hair and fingernails are made.

lateral line—A sense organ along a fish's side.

mammary gland—The part of a mammal's skin that gives off milk.

melanin—A protein that gives skin and hair its color.

molt—To lose feathers or fur.

osteoderm—A grain of bone found in the dermal layers of some animals' skin.

parotoid gland—A gland that releases poison.

pheromone—A scent some animals give off that attracts a mate.

plastron—The lower part of a turtle's shell.

scute—A shield-like bony plate.

sebaceous gland—An oil-producing gland in the dermis.

sebum—An oil given off by a sebaceous gland.

spiracle—An opening to a breathing tube in an insect's or spider's exoskeleton.

subcutaneous layer—The innermost layer of the skin.

undercoat—The fur next to a mammal's body.

FIND OUT MORE

BOOKS

Burnie, David. *Bird*. New York: DK Publishing, 2004.

Clarke, Barry. *Amphibian*. New York: DK Publishing, 2005.

McCarthy, Colin. *Reptile*. New York: DK Publishing, 2000.

Mound, Laurence A. *Insect*. New York: DK Publishing, 2004.

Parker, Steve. *Fish*. London: DK Publishing, 2005.

——. *Human Body*. New York: DK Publishing, 2004.

——. *Mammal*. New York: DK Publishing, 2004.

Stein, Sara Bonnett. *The Evolution Book*. New York: Workman Publishing, 1986.

WEB SITES

The Animal Diversity Web
http://animaldiversity.ummz.umich.edu/site/index.htm
This site contains information about individual species in several different groups of animals, particularly mammals.

Audubon Society
http://www.audubon.org
This organizations is an amazing source of information for people interested in birds and bird-watching.

Cyber School—Marine Life
http://ourworld.compuserve.com/Homepages/jaap/Mmlinks.htm
This site provides information on many fishes and other marine life.

Insecta Inspecta World
http://www.insecta-inspecta.com
This site has all kinds of information about insects.

Neuroscience for Kids—Amazing Animal Senses
http://faculty.washington.edu/chudler/amaze.html
At this site you can learn a lot of amazing facts about animal senses.

INDEX

Page numbers for illustrations are in **boldface.**

ABOUT THE AUTHOR

Sara Swan Miller has enjoyed working with children all her life, first as a Montessori nursery school teacher and later as an outdoor environmental educator at the Mohonk Preserve in New Paltz, New York. As director of the school program, she has taught hundreds of children the importance of appreciating the natural world.

She has written more than fifty books, including *Three Stories You Can Read to Your Dog; Three Stories You Can Read to Your Cat; Three More Stories You Can Read to Your Dog; Three More Stories You Can Read to Your Cat; Three Stories You Can Read to Your Teddy Bear; Will You Sting Me? Will You Bite? The Truth About Some Scary-Looking Insects;* and *What's in the Woods? An Outdoor Activity Book.* She has also written many nonfiction books for children.